ARTIST
TRANSCRIPTIONS
SAXOPHONE

The New Best of
WAYNE SHORTER

Cover Photo: Thomas Dorn

ISBN 0-634-03395-6

HAL•LEONARD®
CORPORATION

7777 W. BLUEMOUND RD. P.O. BOX 13819 MILWAUKEE, WI 53213

Visit Hal Leonard Online at
www.halleonard.com

CONTENTS

Adam's Apple

By Wayne Shorter

All or Nothing at All

Words by Jack Lawrence
Music by Arthur Altman

Ana Maria

By Wayne Shorter

Vamp and Fade

Autumn Leaves
(Les Feuilles Mortes)

English lyric by Johnny Mercer
French lyric by Jacques Prevert
Music by Joseph Kosma

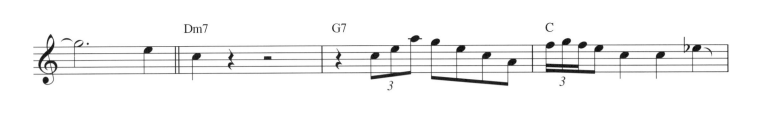

Piano Solo   **63**   2 Choruses   **Bass Solo**   **16**   1/2 Chorus   Head Out
Played by Miles Davis

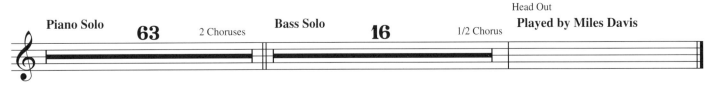

Beauty and the Beast

By Wayne Shorter

Children of the Night

By Wayne Shorter

E.S.P.

By Wayne Shorter

Eighty One

By Miles Davis and Ronald Carter

Face on the Barroom Floor

By Wayne Shorter

Flagships

By Wayne Shorter

Bb Soprano & Tenor Saxophones

Vamp and Fade

Infant Eyes

By Wayne Shorter

Footprints

By Wayne Shorter

If I Were a Bell
from *GUYS AND DOLLS*
By Frank Loesser

Piano Solo
Open
Head Out
Played by Miles Davis

Juju

By Wayne Shorter

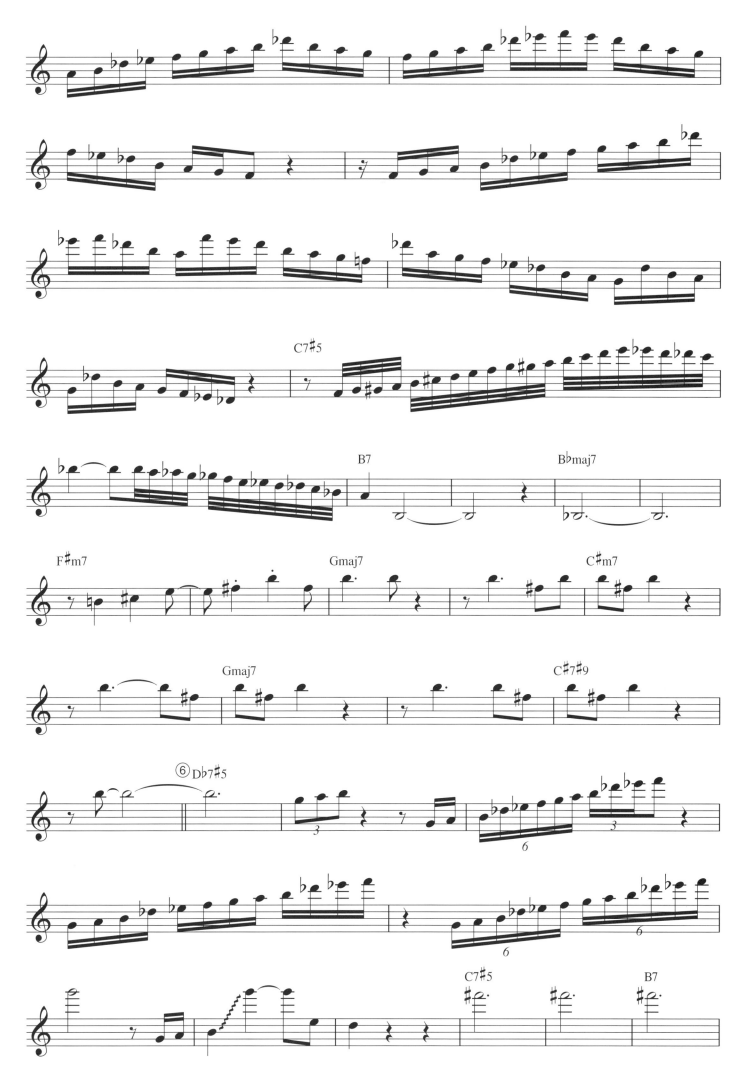

Lester Left Town

By Wayne Shorter

The Last Silk Hat

By Wayne Shorter

B♭ Tenor & Soprano Saxophones

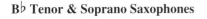

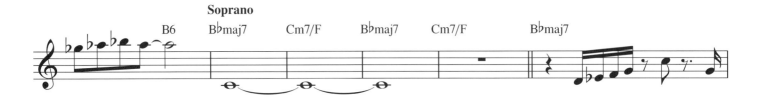

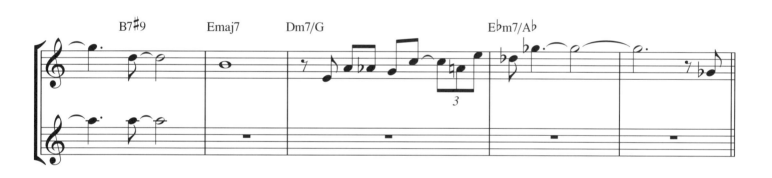

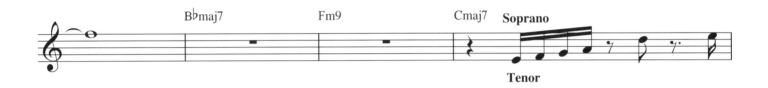

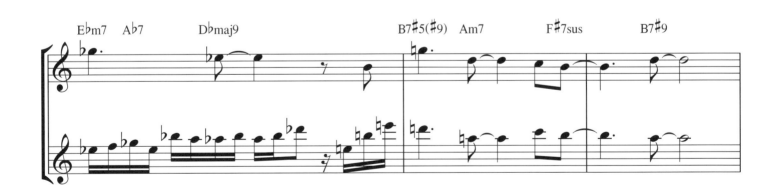

A E7 A B♭ C7   A9

A E7 A B♭ C

Mahjong

By Wayne Shorter

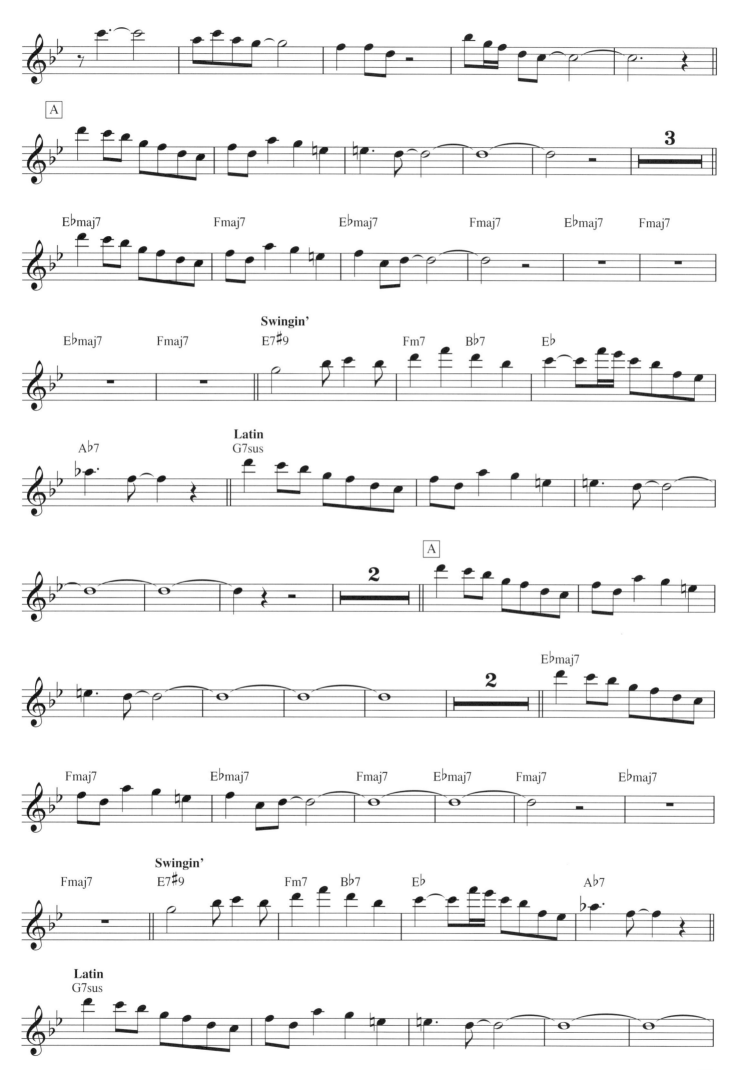

Miyako

By Wayne Shorter

B♭ Tenor Saxophone

82

Masqualero

By Wayne Shorter

Night Dreamer

By Wayne Shorter

This Is for Albert

By Wayne Shorter

*Trumpet, Tenor Sax and Trombone arranged for Tenor Sax.

Penelope

By Wayne Shorter

Speak No Evil

By Wayne Shorter

Virgo

By Wayne Shorter

Water Babies

By Wayne Shorter

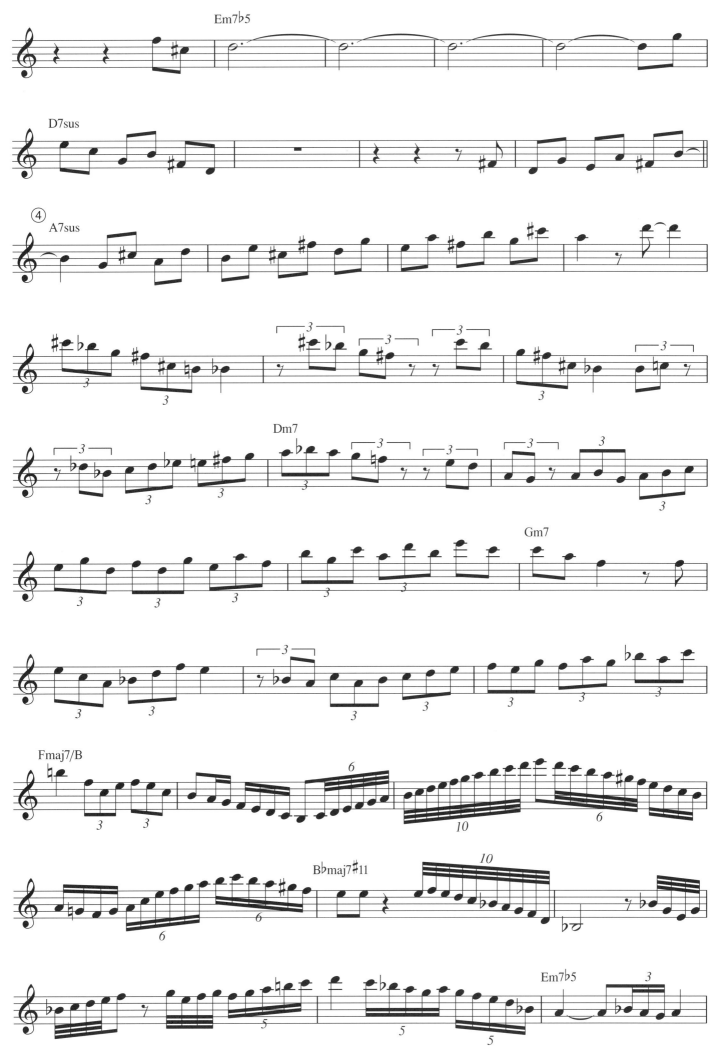

Witch Hunt

By Wayne Shorter

Tom Thumb

By Wayne Shorter